Where in the World Can I . . .

DESIGN A ROBOT?

Where in the World Can I . . .

DESIGN A ROBOT?

WORLD BOOK

www.worldbook.com

World Book, Inc.
180 North LaSalle Street, Suite 900
Chicago, Illinois 60601
USA

For information about other World Book publications, visit our website at **www.worldbook.com** or call **1-800-WORLDBK (967-5325).**

For information about sales to schools and libraries, call 1-800-975-3250 (United States), or 1-800-837-5365 (Canada).

Library of Congress Cataloging-in-Publication Data for this volume has been applied for.

Where in the World Can I...
ISBN: 978-0-7166-5251-9 (set, hc.)

Design a Robot?
ISBN: 978-0-7166-5252-6 (hc.)
ISBN: 978-0-7166-5264-9 (pf.)

Also available as:
ISBN: 978-0-7166-5258-8 (e-book)

STAFF

Editorial
Senior Editor
Shawn Brennan

Curriculum Designer
Caroline Davidson

Proofreader
Nathalie Strassheim

Graphics and Design
Senior Visual Communications Designer
Melanie Bender

Coordinator, Design Development and Production
Brenda Tropinski

Senior Media Editor
Rosalia Bledsoe

Acknowledgments
Writer: Cynthia O'Brien

Produced by
Focus Strategic Communications Inc.

TABLE OF CONTENTS

WHAT IS A ROBOT?

A robot is a machine controlled by a computer. Robots can perform tasks *autonomously* (on their own). But robots only do the jobs or actions that people build and *program* them to do. A program is a set of instructions for a computer to follow. The instructions are written in languages that computers understand. These are electronic languages called *code.*

Knowing how to write code and create programs is key to designing a robot. The other important part is knowing how to build them. This is *engineering*. Engineering uses math and science to design and build things.

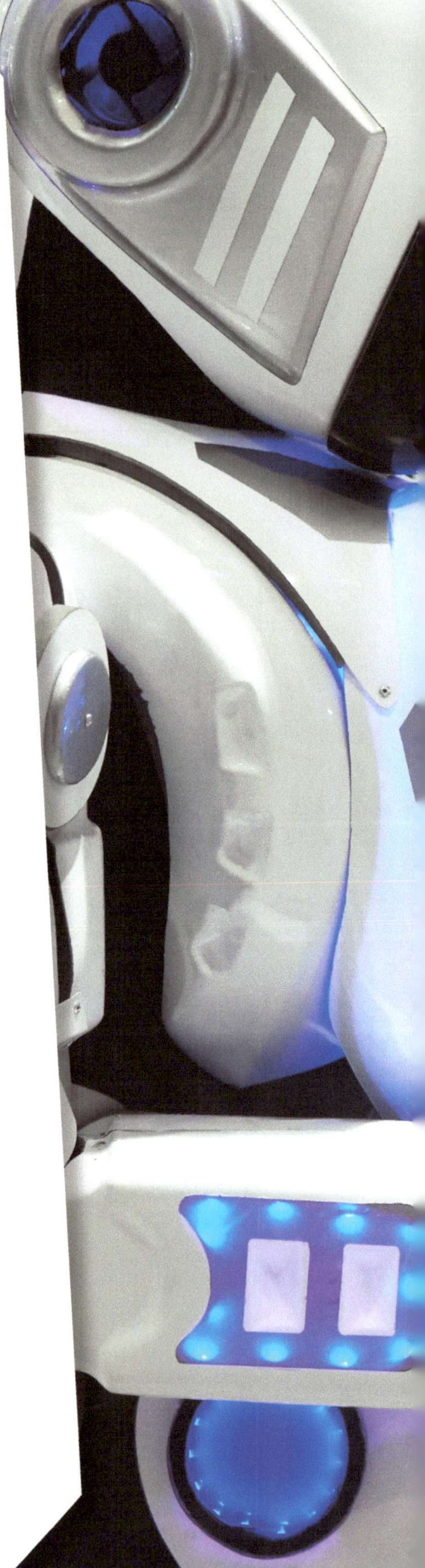

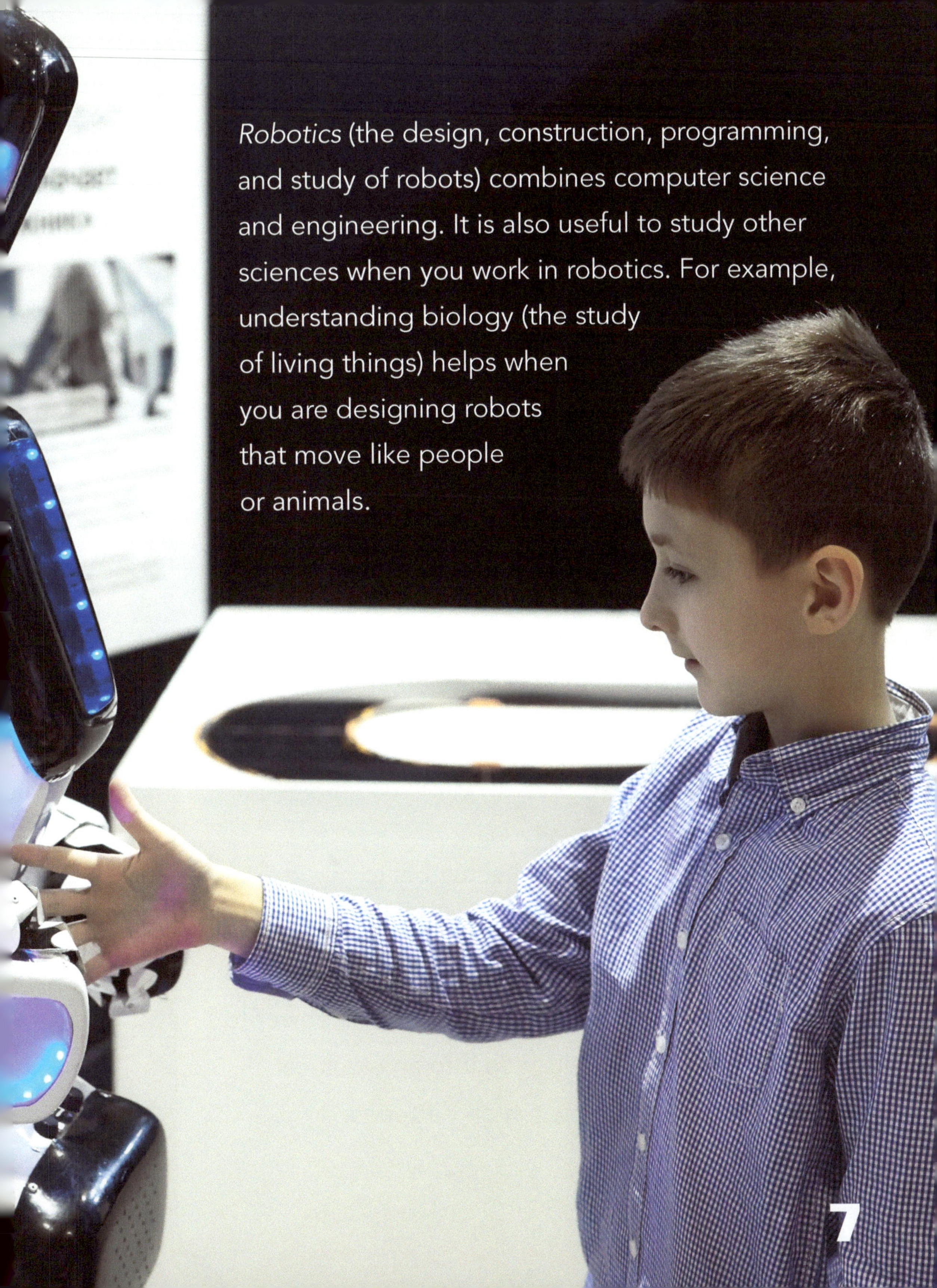

Robotics (the design, construction, programming, and study of robots) combines computer science and engineering. It is also useful to study other sciences when you work in robotics. For example, understanding biology (the study of living things) helps when you are designing robots that move like people or animals.

Humanoid robots are built to look and move like humans. But most robots look nothing like people. Robots are designed to suit the job they need to do. This means they come in all different shapes and sizes. Even so, all robots have a few things in common.

You use your *senses*, such as touch and hearing, to interact with the world. Robots use *sensors* to do the same thing. These are devices that enable robots to detect what is going on around them. Sensors pick up changes in light, motion, sound, and many other things. For example, a robot may have sensors that detect things in its way. It will move to avoid them.

Robots also have parts called *actuators* to move and perform actions. A motor is an actuator. A robot's actuators move its *effectors*. These are such things as grippers, wheels, and arms. Actuators need power to work. Some robots are plugged into an electrical socket. Many other robots run on batteries.

The first robotlike inventions were simple mechanical (relating to machines) devices called *automatons*. The ancient Chinese made automatons in the 200's B.C. In the late 1400's, the Italian artist and inventor Leonardo da Vinci drew plans for a mechanical knight (armored soldier). Later Europeans created automatons using clockwork pieces. These automatons were often shaped like people and could play music, draw, or write.

The word "robot" was first used in 1921. It appeared in the play *Rossum's Universal Robots* (*R.U.R.*) by Czech writer Karel Čapek *(KAR uhl CHAH pehk)*. In the 1950's, George Devol invented the first *industrial* (to do with the making of goods and services) robot. It was developed into a robotic arm called Unimate. In the 1960's, robots like these were installed in many car factories.

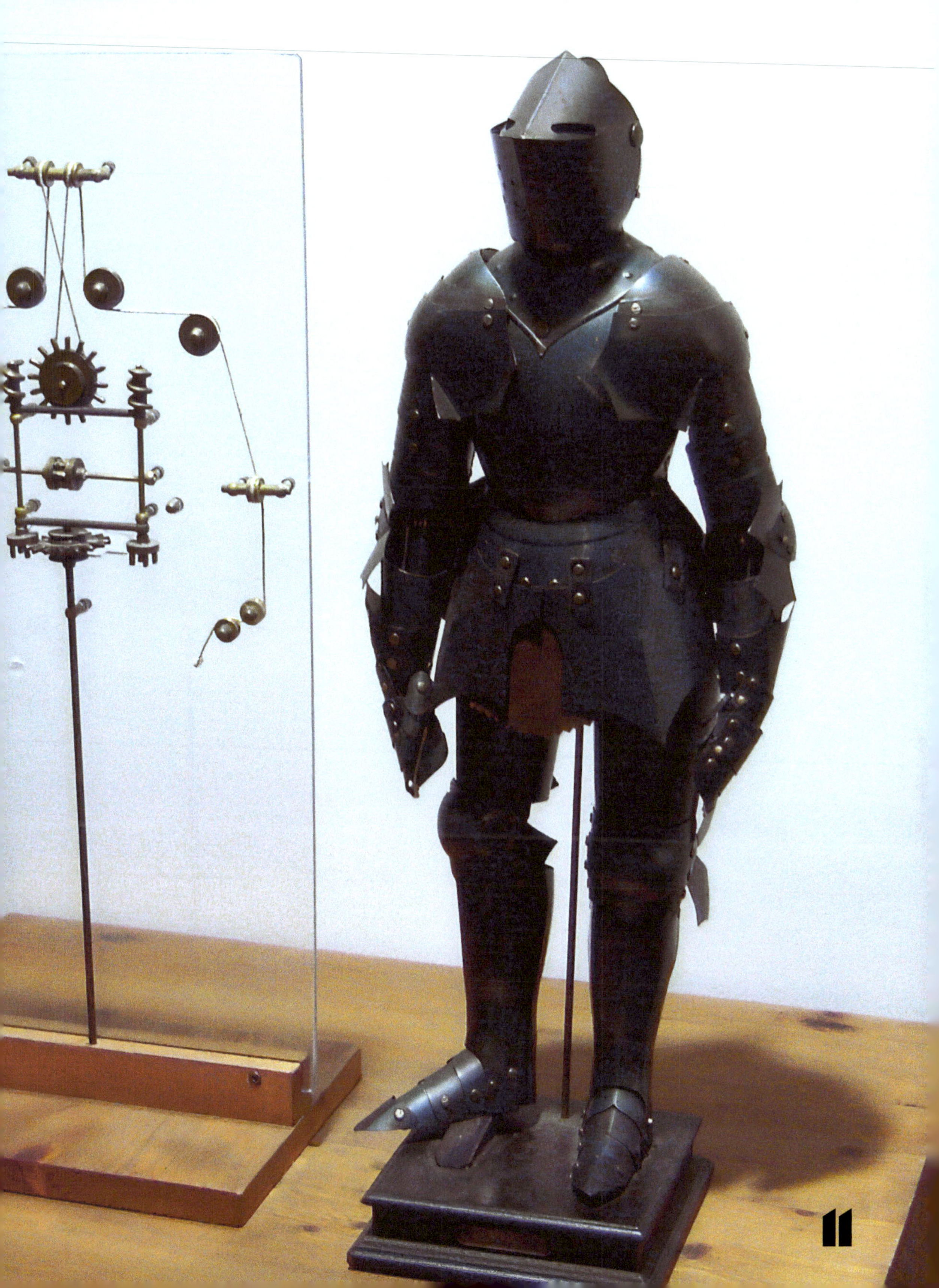

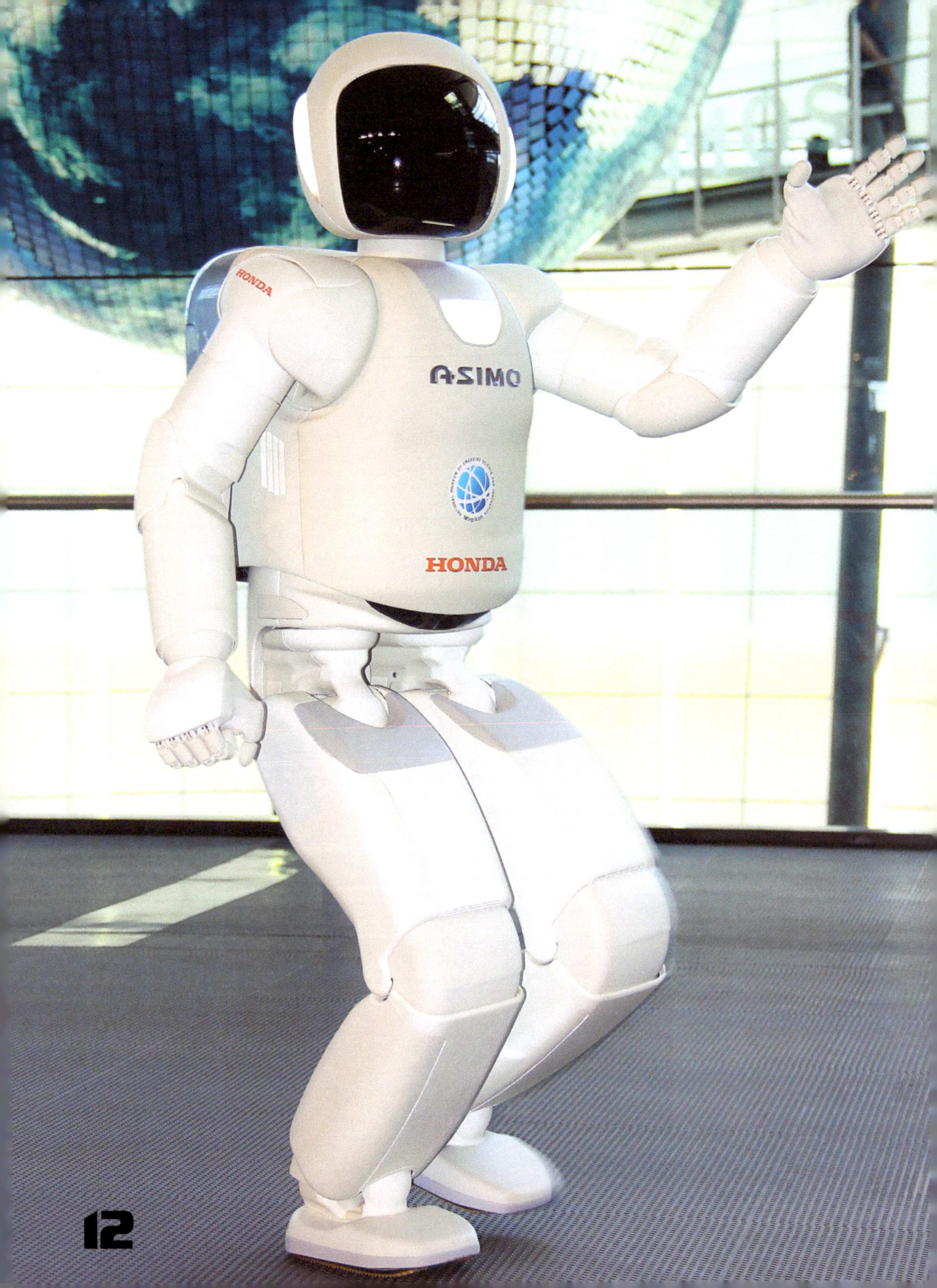
HONDA
ASIMO
HONDA

Robots launched into space with Sputnik I, in 1957. Back on Earth, engineers at Stanford University, California, were working on *mobile* (capable of moving around) robots. In the late 1960's, they built Shakey. The tall robot had cameras and touch sensors and shook when it moved. The computer that controlled Shakey was the size of a room!

As computer science developed, computers became smaller and able to do much more. Robots have become more sophisticated, too. NASA's Pathfinder rover landed on Mars in 1997. Meanwhile, there were advances in humanoid robots. Japan introduced the first ASIMO in 2000. This humanoid robot could run, dance, and recognize faces.

In 2016, a robotics company in Hong Kong launched Sophia, a realistic-looking humanoid robot.

Today, robots are all around us. At home, there are robot vacuum cleaners that gather dust and crumbs from around the house. Robot lawn mowers keep the grass trimmed. Robot pets are fun to play with. Aibo first came out in 1999. Newer robot pets look even more lifelike. Your school might have robots that help with teaching.

All kinds of workplaces use robots. Many robots do *repetitive* jobs. This means they can do the same task over and over again. They make work easier for people. Industries, such as car factories, use robots to put machines together.

In hospitals, robot nurses can take samples to a lab, fetch medical supplies, or carry clean bedding.

Delivery robots can bring you your groceries and other packages. They can also take medical supplies to remote (far away) or difficult-to-reach places.

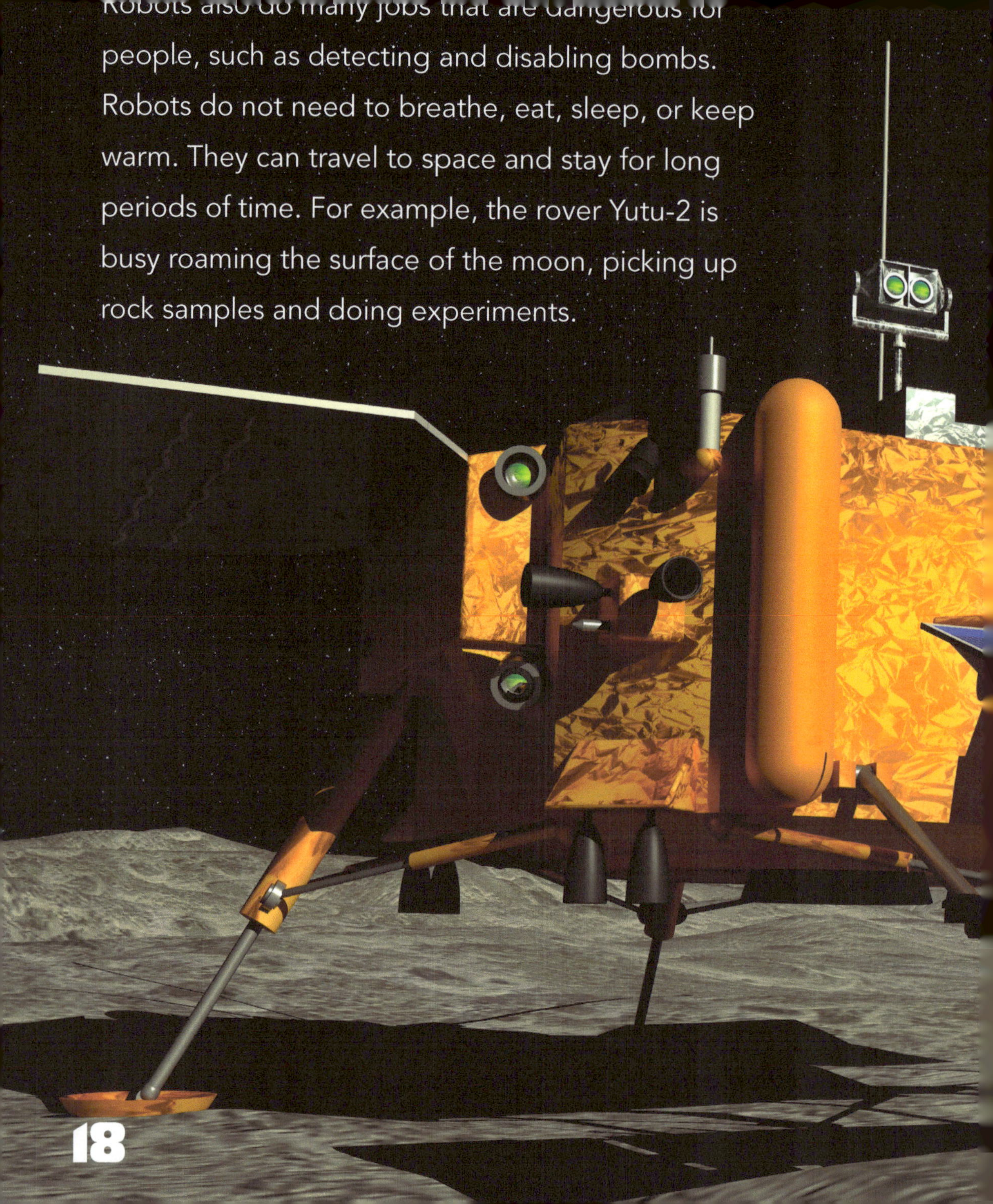

Robots also do many jobs that are dangerous for people, such as detecting and disabling bombs. Robots do not need to breathe, eat, sleep, or keep warm. They can travel to space and stay for long periods of time. For example, the rover Yutu-2 is busy roaming the surface of the moon, picking up rock samples and doing experiments.

Robots are helping scientists with research on Earth, too. Robot fish swim in the ocean and collect information about real sea life. Other robots go deep underwater to explore the ocean floor. A small robot called ECHO lives with emperor penguins in Antarctica and sends information back to scientists. In the lab, robots do experiments alongside scientists. Robots are even helping to save the planet. They can sort materials for recycling or help detect pollution in the air and water.

What could robots do in the future? They already serve dinner and cook food in some restaurants. One day, robots could be cooking food in your kitchen! They may do more of your household chores, too.

Robotics engineers and scientists are working on robots that can fight fires. They are designing robotic *exoskeletons* (skeletons on the outside) to help injured people stand and walk. Fully self-driving cars (with no driver control) and trucks may be the transportation of the future.

Artificial intelligence (AI) will also change robots. AI is the ability for devices, like computers, to think and behave like people. An AI robot may be able to learn to do new things on its own and solve more difficult problems.

Cobots are robots that work alongside people, like CIMON that works with astronauts. AI robots of the future may interact even more with people. Natural language processing (NLP) will allow robots to understand and communicate in human languages.

Are you a future roboticist? There are plenty of ways to get started. STEM (science, technology, engineering, and math) classes at school will give you some basics. Many schools also have robotics classes or after-school robotics clubs. You can also attend online camps to learn more about coding and designing robots.

LEGO Mindstorms® kits let you design and build your own robots. The kits use special LEGO pieces and come with instructions for coding. Once you sharpen your skills, you can sign up for robotics events, such as the FIRST Robotics Competition.

In the meantime, read on to find out where you can design and build your very own robot.

When you are older, you can study robotics at colleges and universities. There are many to choose from, but here are a few:

Carnegie Mellon University—Pittsburgh, Pennsylvania, USA

ETH Zürich—Zürich, Switzerland

Swiss Federal Institute of Technology Lausanne—Lausanne, Switzerland

Harbin Institute of Technology (HIT)—Harbin, Heilongjiang, China

Massachusetts Institute of Technology (MIT)—Cambridge, Massachusetts, USA

Stanford University—Stanford, California, USA

University of Freiburg—Baden-Württemberg, Germany

University of Oxford—Oxford, United Kingdom

The University of Tokyo—Tokyo, Japan

THE TECH INTERACTIVE

The Tech Interactive, or "The Tech," is a technology center in downtown San Jose, California. San Jose is in the famous Silicon Valley, home to such technology giants as Google. The Tech Museum of *Innovation* (a new idea, method, or device) first opened in 1990 and moved to a much larger, more colorful building in 1998.

In 2019, the museum changed its name to The Tech *Interactive*. An interactive museum is one that involves actions between visitors and the exhibits. So, instead of just looking at exhibits, you can touch, create, listen, and more.

When you visit The Tech, start your tour at the Solve for Earth exhibit. Here you can find out about new technologies that will help to save our planet. For example, new building materials may pull harmful carbon and pollution from the air. What jobs could robots do that will help protect Earth?

The Social Robots gallery is The Tech's robot design hub. Here you will design, build, and program your very own robot. The Tech has different sensors, actuators, and effectors for you to use. Friendly staff are there to help you along the way.

To begin, head to one of the many computer stations in this section. You can choose one of many robot options on the computer. For example, you can design and build a robot that can plant trees. The robots start with color-coded base parts. This helps you to add the other parts, such as motion sensors, in the right places.

Once your robot has all its working parts, there are hats, hair, and other pieces to make it look good, too.

Next, meet a robot in the Animaker exhibit. Then interact with the robot to learn how artificial intelligence and machines can work together. You will build an animal using LEGO bricks and scan it with a 3-D scanner. Make it your own by changing its colors and choosing movements. Then your animal will appear in the digital jungle on the screen. You are teaching the computer as you go!

If space robots are your thing, check out the Space Exploration gallery. Space agencies around the world have robotics experts designing and building new robots all the time. At The Tech, you can experience the thrill of interacting with a Mars rover.

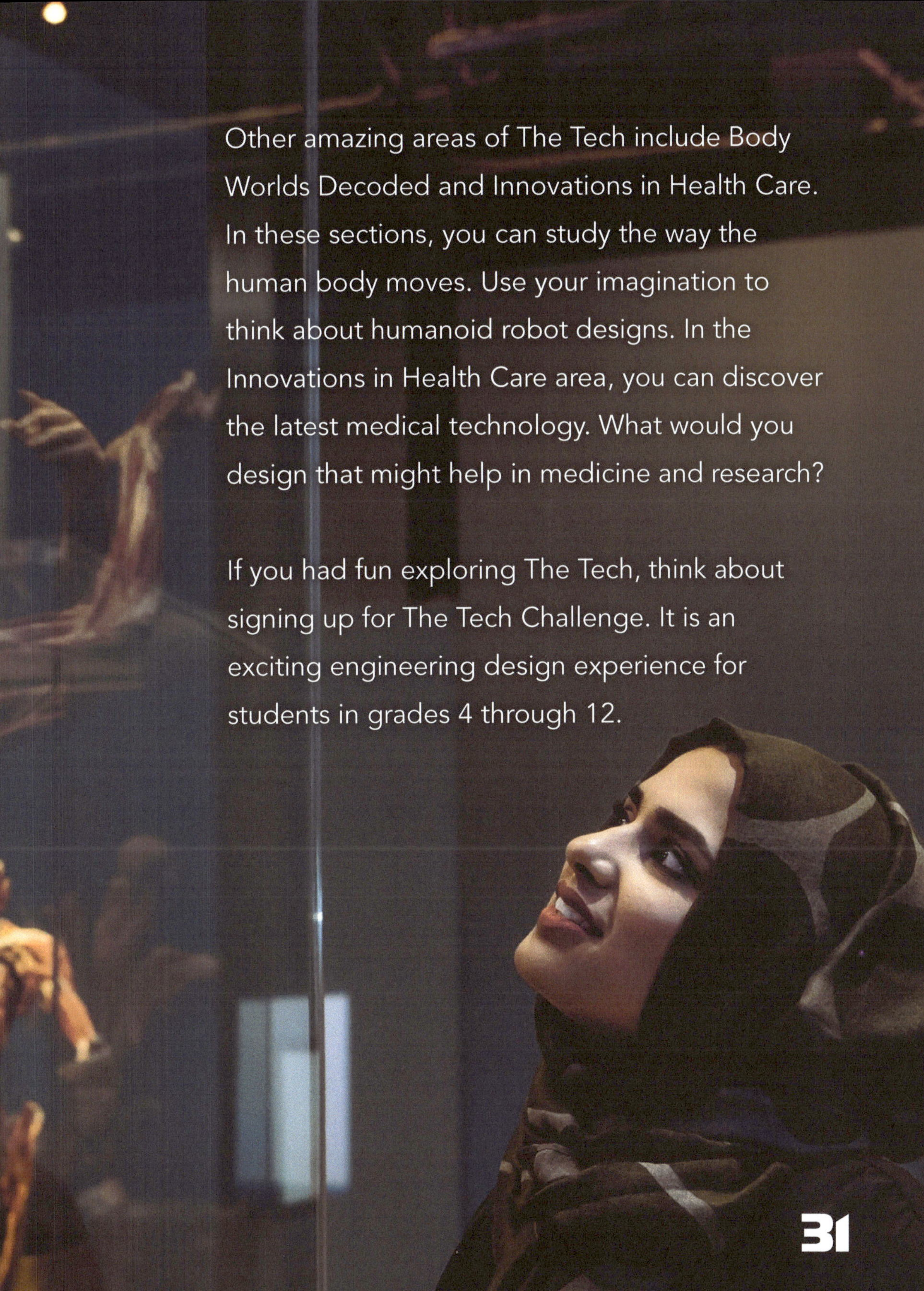

Other amazing areas of The Tech include Body Worlds Decoded and Innovations in Health Care. In these sections, you can study the way the human body moves. Use your imagination to think about humanoid robot designs. In the Innovations in Health Care area, you can discover the latest medical technology. What would you design that might help in medicine and research?

If you had fun exploring The Tech, think about signing up for The Tech Challenge. It is an exciting engineering design experience for students in grades 4 through 12.

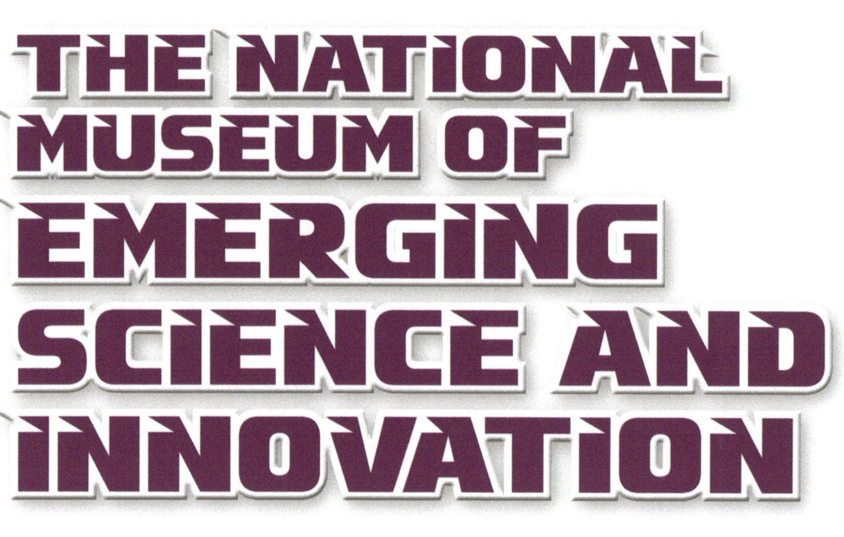

THE NATIONAL MUSEUM OF EMERGING SCIENCE AND INNOVATION

Robots are the star attractions of the National Museum of Emerging Science and Innovation. This science museum, known as Miraikan, is in Tokyo, Japan. Miraikan means "hall of the future." To get to the museum, you take a monorail over the Rainbow Bridge to Odaiba, an artificially created island in Tokyo Bay.

A giant model of Earth is a spectacular sight when you enter Miraikan. The model has 10,362 display panels that give visitors a vivid, realistic picture of our Earth today. From here, head to the third floor to visit the robots.

The Create Your Future zone is all about robots from the past and the future. Have a look at the timeline on the wall to see how robots have changed and developed over the years. Miraikan features some of the latest robots built in Japan.

The Robots in Your Life exhibit will show you many of the ways that we already live with robots. It also challenges visitors to question how we will live with robots in the future. What roles will robots play, and what new kinds of robots will there be?

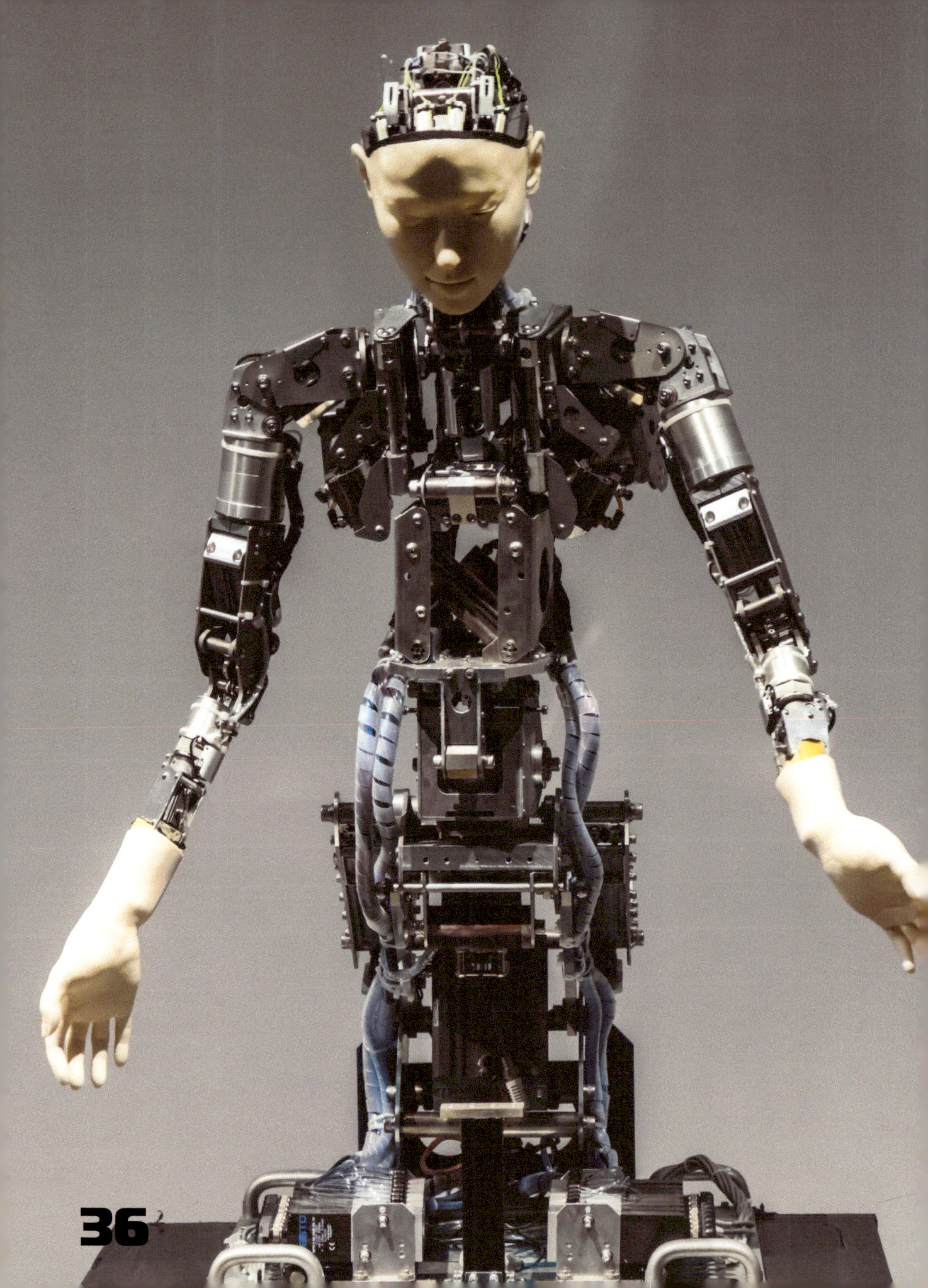

Androids are the focus in the Android: What is Human? exhibit. Androids are humanoid robots, and some are amazingly lifelike. One of the robots, called Alter, has its mechanical parts on display. Its face and hands are covered in a material called silicon, so it looks like skin. Alter does not have robot legs, so it sits on top of a cube. The robot performs for visitors.

In June 2022, scientists at the University of Tokyo revealed that they have grown humanlike skin on a robotic finger. This may enable roboticists to make robots that look even more like people.

Find out what it would be like to hang out with the robots at the International Space Station (ISS). Miraikan features a *replica* (copy) of part of the ISS that visitors can tour.

Robotics scientists are hard at work at the Miraikan. The people working on the Intelligent Systems Project are studying how robots might exist alongside humans and even make their own decisions. Other projects include one that focuses on communication. Will robots be able to interact with humans in a more meaningful way?

Miraikan's Open Lab event allows visitors to take part in demonstrations and research studies. Here you will discover the latest in AI. You may even be able to take part in a robot experiment!

iD TECH CAMPS

At robotics camps, you will learn how to program and design your very own robot! The iD Tech Camps hold summer sessions all over the United States and in some other countries, such as China. For students who cannot attend in person, iD Tech also offers online camps. Whichever camp you choose, there is plenty of fun to be had.

In-person camps are held on campuses of some of the best universities and colleges. These institutions do not run the camps, but some of them offer the best education in robotics. When you are older, you might even attend one of them! Camp locations include the Massachusetts Institute of Technology (MIT), Carnegie Mellon University, and Stanford University. While at camp, you will have a chance to tour the campus where you are based. Also, when you are not in the tech lab, you can take part in loads of outdoor activities.

When considering iD Tech, have a look at the different camps they offer. For example, there are camps just for girls aged 10 to 15 years old. These camps enable girls to share ideas and work together on projects.

There are two-week coding and AI camps for older children aged 13 to 18. Other week-long camps are divided into age groups, with different courses available in each one. There are camps for students aged 7 to 9 years, 10 to 12 years, and 13 to 17 years.

Coding is a big part of the camp experience. Camps for the younger age group focus on writing code with JavaScript.

If you are in the middle age group, you will code with JavaScript, but also learn the basics of Python. Python is one of the most used coding languages today.

What else will you do at iD Tech Camp? One special course for the younger campers is visual coding. You will learn to use Scratch, a programming language developed by the MIT Media Lab. See what you can teach a robot to do!

Once you understand Scratch, you can go further and explore *virtual* (online or on a computer screen, rather than in real life) robotics.

Older campers learn about AI and robots. They also learn how to design and build a robot by using what they have learned about coding.

Working in teams, campers program their robots to do different tasks. They choose the appropriate sensors and effectors, depending on those tasks.

For example, robots may have to get around a *maze*. A maze is an area that includes different pathways, so you can get lost very easily. When all the robots are ready, the teams take part in a robotics competition.

READING FOCUS

Text Structure is all about the way a text is organized. When we know the structure, we can focus more of our energy and attention on comprehending what we read.

This book uses a Description Text Structure. It describes a topic and its characteristics using details, adjectives, and a logical order. Description texts often use examples to show and explain the main idea or topic.

Description texts usually include a lot of interesting details. We can use a graphic organizer to help us keep track of the most important information.

Prove It!

Find at least 3 examples from the text that support the claim that this book uses a Description Text Structure.

1. This is a Bubble Diagram, a strong graphic organizer for Description texts. Visit **www.worldbook.com/resources** to download and print copies or create your own!
2. As you read and/or revisit the text, complete a Bubble Diagram for EACH section:
   - What Is a Robot?
   - The Tech Interactive
   - The National Museum of Emerging Science and Innovation
   - iD Tech Camps
3. For each section, write the title in the center-most bubble. Next, add important details to the bubbles attached to that central, main idea. Remember, you do not have enough bubbles for *every* detail. Think critically to determine which details to include.

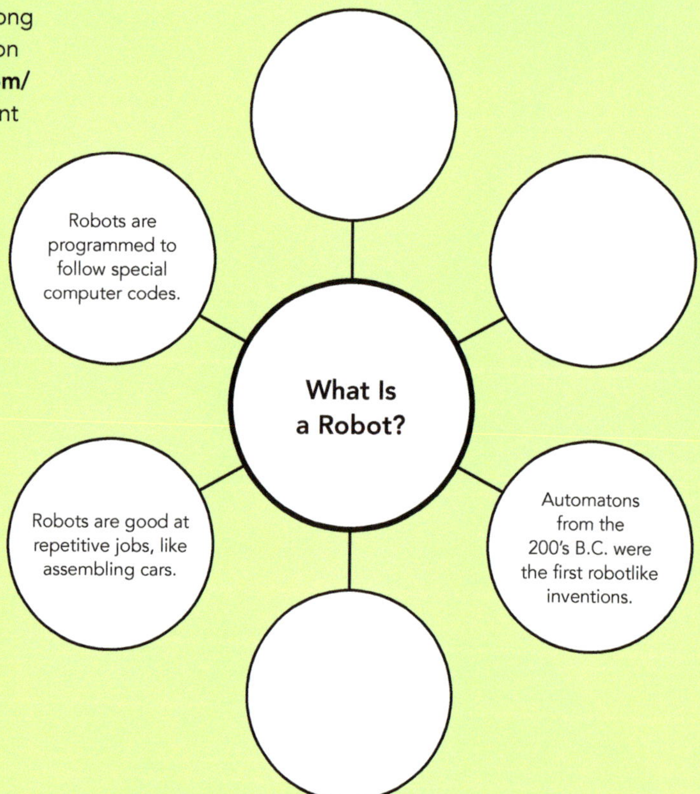

What other information about designing robots will you add to your Bubble Diagram?

WRITING FOCUS

What do YOU think?

In your opinion, which of the three spotlighted locations would be best for designing a robot?

Review the notes you took on your Bubble Diagrams. Use evidence from the text, supported by logical reasoning, to answer the question. Your writing should include:

- A **hook** where you grab your readers' attention
- A **thesis statement** where you state your opinion
- At least 3 **reasons** why that is your opinion
- At least 3 **details** that support each reason

Use an Opinion Writing Graphic Organizer to sort through your thoughts before you write your response. Create your own or download and print a version from **www.worldbook.com/resources.**

Opinion Writing Graphic Organizer

Hook and Thesis:	Reason #1	Detail #1
		Detail #2
		Detail #3
	Reason #2	Detail #1
		Detail #2
		Detail #3
	Reason #3	Detail #1
		Detail #2
		Detail #3

You might have noticed some words in this book written in *italics*. That means they are vocabulary terms! **Challenge yourself!** Can you include at least 5 of these words in your opinion writing?

INDEX

ACKNOWLEDGMENTS

Cover: © Try My Best/Shutterstock
TP: © Gorodenkoff, Shutterstock
6–7 © SergeyKlopotov, Shutterstock
8–9 © MikeDotta, Shutterstock
10–11 Christoph Roser (CC BY-SA 4.0); © agefotostock, Alamy
12–13 © Khliustina Ekaterina, Shutterstock; © paparazzza, Shutterstock
14–15 © Kim Kyung-Hoon, Alamy; © Alex_Traksel, Shutterstock
16–17 © SariMe, Shutterstock; © atiger, Shutterstock
18–19 © Alejo Miranda, Shutterstock
20–21 © Nippon News, Alamy; © ZUMA Press, Alamy
22–23 © VisualArtStudio, Shutterstock
24–25 © The Tech Interactive
26–27 © The Tech Interactive
28–29 © The Tech Interactive
30–31 © The Tech Interactive
32–33 © Manassavee Rukhavibul, Shutterstock
34–35 © Nippon News, Alamy; © Cowardlion, Dreamstime
36–37 © Steve Vidler, Alamy; © Jae C. Hong, Associated Press
38–39 © Nippon News, Alamy
40–41 © svetikd, iStockPhoto
42–43 © Monkey Business Images, Shutterstock
44–45 © Blackout Footage, Shutterstock

www.ingramcontent.com/pod-product-compliance
Ingram Content Group UK Ltd.
Pitfield, Milton Keynes, MK11 3LW, UK
UKHW060102300726
14090UKWH00003B/353

* 9 7 8 0 7 1 6 6 5 2 6 4 9 *